Dear Lord,
Who Am I Really?

Journey to a True Self-Image – Book 1

Joan Clickner

This book has been published under the supervision of Prophet Del Hall III and by F.U.N. Inc. the parent company of Guidance for a Better Life.

Edited by Lorraine Fortier, Del Hall IV, David Hughes, and Terry Kisner. Cover Photo by Jill Wellington. Cover Design by Del Hall IV.

No part of this publication may be reproduced, stored in or introduced into a retrieval system, or transmitted, in any form or by any means (electronically, mechanical, photocopying, recording or otherwise), without the prior written permission of both the copyright owner and the publisher of this book. Re-selling through electronic outlets (like Amazon, Barnes and Noble or eBay) without permission of the publisher is illegal and punishable by law. The scanning, uploading, and distribution of this book via the Internet or via any other means without the permission of the publisher is illegal and punishable by law. Please purchase only authorized editions and do not participate in or encourage electronic piracy of copyrightable materials. Your support of the author's right is appreciated.

Copyright © 2017 F.U.N. Inc. All rights reserved.

ISBN: 978-0-9982218-0-9

ABOUT THE AUTHOR

Joan Clickner was one of those people forever struggling to know her life's dream and still wondering as an adult what she wanted to be when she grew up. After receiving a bachelor's degree in English she did international charity work, and later found various part-time jobs from catering to proofreading while raising a family. For the past several years she has served as office manager for a local goldsmith.

Finally comfortable in her own skin, Joan is now studying for a master's degree to take her into a new career of health and wellness coaching. She lives with her husband, two children, and two cuddly dogs in Charlottesville, Virginia.

Joan credits the spiritual teachings and loving guidance she receives from Prophet Del Hall III at Guidance for a Better Life for her miraculous transformation.

Table of Contents

1. A New Dream..1
2. Just Listen..4
3. The Root of My False Self-Image............9
4. Where Do I Stand Now?.........................12
5. Reassurance I Can Do This....................16
6. Healing With My Father.........................19
7. First Rays of Light.................................21
8. Guilt From a Past Life and a
   Heartfelt Prayer...................................24
9. Beginning to Open My Wings..............28
10. Removing Blocks Between Myself
    And God...30
11. Passing of My Father..........................35
12. Comforting My Mother.......................39
13. The Light Grows Stronger..................42
14. Awaiting the Harvest..........................45
15. Sweet Victory....................................48
16. A Green Light to Serve.......................56

17. No More Digging Up the Past............59
18. The Shorts of Truth...........................63
19. Changing Outside and In..................68
20. Self-Reverence................................71
21. I Am Worthy of God's Love...............75
22. Forgiving My Past............................77
23. Attached to My Story.......................84
24. Clarity at Spirit Week.......................87
25. Checkmate.....................................92
26. Comfortable In My Own Skin.............95

Appendix

Guidance for a Better Life "Our Story"......97
    My Father's Journey (Del Hall III)..........97
    My Son, Del Hall IV........................109
What is the Role of God's Prophet?..........113
HU — An Ancient Name for God............121
Articles of Faith................................123
Contact Information............................137
Additional Reading.............................138

1

A New Dream

You know that dream where find yourself back in school with a big test to take, but you haven't been to any of the classes, you haven't done any of the assignments, and you're totally unprepared for it? And you're so relieved to wake up and find out it was just a dream. I had this dream for years and years. In my case, the dream eventually took on more detail; it was now a history class and I was shocked and dismayed to discover I was enrolled in it. The class was hard, the subject dry, and I really wasn't interested in it. But I didn't want to fail, either. The teacher, a dim, cold figure in the background, offered no support or empathy as I scrambled to catch on and catch up.

Recently I had a new dream: I was going to a school where a number of women "in recovery" were enrolled. The colors of the place were warm and sundrenched, compared to the dreary grays of the other dream. I was a student but also helping others get back on their feet and take advantage of the education they'd long been wanting. I was enrolled in surfing lessons and dance classes, and could hardly wait to get started. And I was specifically informed by an administrator: You do not have to attend that history class anymore. Hallelujah!

Dreams can be hard to interpret but these ones were very clear. The unsupportive, judgmental professor was part of me and how I viewed myself. The history class was my personal history that I didn't want to spend more time rehashing. The new dream shows me having turned a corner. I'm leaving my past behind. I'm transforming and helping others do the same. Surfing and dance are joyful activities symbolizing living in the here and now, not dwelling in the past. In the dream, I was excused from the history class. God is telling me I do not need to focus on my past mistakes and failings. Get out and live!

How did I turn the corner? How did I leave a life of self-judgment and self-inflicted pain and start living? Looking back, I can see a thousand moments, a thousand gifts from God, placed around me to teach and sustain me on my way, to give me the strength and tools to change. It reminds me of hiking in the Alps as a child with family one summer. It was hard for us kids, being mostly uphill. We'd round a curve in the path and there would be a couple of succulent apricots waiting on a boulder, placed there by my aunt to give us a little energy and encouragement as we followed her a few yards back. God placed so many things in my path to help me get where I wanted to go.

2
Just Listen

To pick a spot to start my story, I will go to January 2014, at this point about two and a half years ago. I was attending a weekend retreat at Guidance for a Better Life. The idea of these two-day retreats is to review, refresh, clarify, and build on experiences from the summer weeklong retreat. Our teacher, Prophet Del Hall, stopped me at some point in the weekend and suggested it would benefit me to just be quiet. Not just that weekend, but for awhile. Like a year or so. To stop talking, to listen to the other students who might have a bigger spiritual skillset than I did. I don't know if you've ever experienced something like this but you can imagine it: Someone takes you by both shoulders and says, "Stop. Just stop. Take a breath. You're making it worse. Breathe. Slow down. Okay." It's a relief when it happens. It's a blessing. I thank God for it.

So what was happening that had Del do this? I think he just saw my mad scramble to "do it right." When you basically feel deep down like you're no good, like you need to change NOW, like you're going to be left behind, lose everything, be exposed as the fraud you are, you scramble. Harder and harder. You're down in a pit you made yourself and clawing at the muddy side, which is getting slicker and slicker from your efforts. Each failure to get out weakens you. At some point you're ready to give up. Del saw all this and figuratively placed his hands on my shoulders. Stop struggling. Start over.

I'm not sure what I looked like to most people at this time, but I suspect it would take a pretty perceptive person to see my inner torment. I went through life cracking jokes and smiling at people, trying to be a pleasing employee, wife, and mother of two. I worked hard to avoid criticism. I tried to look good at all times. I think I spent an inordinate amount of time trying to avoid making mistakes, and I avoided any real risk. Which meant I wasn't living life. And I was worn out. If you saw me in the evening, I was staring at the TV. The phone would ring and I would glare over my shoulder at it. Doesn't anyone know I am done with the world at 8:00pm? I couldn't stand any more contact with things that might hurt. So I hid. My sphere of living grew smaller and smaller. So many things had the potential to hurt and had to be avoided, and the list kept growing.

At one time I had lived a pretty adventurous life; at its pinnacle I traveled to Kenya as a twenty-three-year-old and spent a year living and working in the dangerous city of Nairobi. But after that push my energy started to dwindle to a point, years later, where to answer the phone or finish doing the dishes without a break was hard. In my efforts to avoid pain my energy had drained to nothing.

At Guidance for a Better Life, which is all about learning to manifest your Divine nature, I was the same as I was everywhere else. Trying to say the right thing, look good, be safe from criticism. How does this work in a place devoted to helping you becoming your true self? Not well. When you want to grow spiritually but you can't be open it causes real wear and tear. I was so mad at myself for my behavior that I beat myself up over it, and that wasn't helping. Believe me, I had used willpower to try to overcome my fearful, shrinking, self-defeating attitude. I had tried to act bold, I had tried to feel bold. I had repeated things to myself I knew were true, like, "God loves me. I am worthy of God's Love. I accept your love, God," but it didn't feel like it was touching me. I still felt basically unworthy and incompetent. And I didn't love myself. I knew all this was wrong — I am a child of God and as Soul I am boundless and capable — but I didn't know how to stop feeling bad about myself. So Del's instruction to be quiet at his retreat center was a gift from God. I needed to stop scrambling up that muddy wall and exhausting the last of my energy.

I knew right away this quiet time wasn't forever, and it wasn't dormancy; I wasn't to do nothing. In fact, it would be quite active. This would be a time of profound change for me. I didn't know what it would look like, but I knew if I were vigilant I would perceive important gifts of insight as well as tools for implementing those insights in practical ways. The pressure to speak (in my mind the pressure to perform) was off, leaving me with room to explore, to listen, to really hear what God was teaching.

3
The Root of My False Self-Image

So what was wrong, what was I like? What was this false self I believed in so strongly that it was basically keeping me small and scared? Where did it come from? I do think it's important to look at one's past and see where these beliefs come from. When you do, you can have freedom from them. You can make peace with the past, with your own mistakes and people who might have hurt you. Forgiveness of self and others is key to leaving the past in the past instead of dragging it all over with you. This usually happens in stages. A chunk of regret falls off here, and slab of resentment there. Then you realize there's more, a different texture, a different area. It can't be forced but it is entirely necessary for moving through your life freely.

In my case, my false self was developed not only in this lifetime but in past lives. A great piece of it was rooted in the very distant past, in a lifetime where I felt I completely failed as a wife, mother, and servant of God. I was also hurt by others in that life and felt angry and wronged, but mostly I blamed myself. I deeply regretted my carelessness and poor judgment in allowing myself to end up among people who hurt me and my loved ones. I carried a huge amount of shame into this lifetime for what I did back then.

While how I was raised in this lifetime contributed to my fear of putting a foot wrong, my deep shame, my lack of love for self; those were much older. If I had had parents who made zero mistakes, it would still have been there. I am grateful to have grown up in the family I did, which brought these long-established beliefs about myself to the surface so I could see them and eventually address them. But this is a much more recent view, and one of the many gifts to come out of the process I've come through. For a long time I blamed my upbringing, and my father in particular, for how terrible I felt about myself. And I blamed myself even more for being simply no good to begin with.

At the start of my quiet time at Guidance for a Better Life, these views were beyond my control. But now I could work on disentangling from them without the desperation that only makes a tangle worse. To be more accurate here, I should say I received a healing from God. A healing over time, bit by bit, in God's time by His Grace, with His Prophet's guidance, and through my effort.

4

Where Do I Stand Now?

While I attend retreats at Guidance for a Better Life several times a year, the majority of my time is, of course, spent out and about in my daily life. This quiet time, I should explain, did not just mean not speaking up in classes. It meant taking a step back and observing instead of acting, or reacting, in my everyday life, in everything I did. To create a quiet observer and listener in me. You could say, watch and listen as Soul, my true self, or to at least try. And figure out with the help of the inner Prophet what I was doing — and why — so I could make real changes.

Here's where I started in January 2014. A description of how I saw myself:

- "A perpetual botcher." This means I felt

whatever opportunity came along I was sure to screw it up, at least in part.

- A feeling of griminess. I had felt this way at least back into my early teens. Like I had a gray film over all of my being I could do nothing to remove.

- I felt defeated. A failure. Heavy.

- I felt harsh, mean, and selfish.

- I had a total inability to think or speak clearly under pressure.

Elaborating on this last bullet, I often found I couldn't articulate what I was thinking; my speaking didn't reflect the wisdom and intelligence I often saw in myself. Stupid things kept coming out of my mouth. Or I'd have blocked thinking — no access to thoughts I knew were in there somewhere. This problem contributed to my already massive lack of self-confidence.

I carried always a sense of shame and

unworthiness. And no amount of reminding myself that God loved me or that I was Soul seemed to help. God might love me, I thought, but I was a screw-up, and I was a screw-up for seeing myself as a screw-up, because enlightened people saw themselves with compassion. God might love me, but I felt like that was just because he had to, because he had to love all His children, even the losers.

When you don't feel worthy of God's Love, you don't draw nigh to Him. I picture God offering a well of Divine water, nourishing and refreshing. When you don't love yourself, you don't push your way through the crowd to get your share of it. You hang back, maybe you take a little when the crowd subsides. A few anemic sips. But you are not hearty about it, you do not strive for it. By the fact that I am here, though, that I didn't just perish, I know I was receiving something. I wouldn't have survived without

God's Love sustaining me. Yet another part of me trusted that somewhere in me there was a vigorous, beautiful person and through this quiet time, I prayed fervently, I would have access to her.

5
Reassurance I Can Do This

After that January retreat I had a dream of paddling a canoe down a path with someone I knew upon waking was the inner Prophet. Big waves washed over us and I braced with each one, but we never capsized. The canoe filled up with water and Prophet instructed me to bail it. As a ten-year-old in summer camp long ago we were taught how two people could empty a swamped canoe by turning it upside down, then swimming underneath to lift and flip it. I don't think my fellow campers and I ever succeeded, but in my dream I did with Prophet's help. Together we lifted the canoe and dumped out the water, then righted it again. I saw it was full of big cracks and was amazed it could still float. The skin was worn but not the frame — waves had worn off the old skin, rotted by time, and it needed replacing. But the frame was just fine.

I knew Prophet gave me this dream to show me where I stood and to fortify my hope that I could do this. The real me was fine, the outer self was worn out and in need of renewal. Personal effort was required in this transformation, and I had skills beyond what I might realize. The waves swamping our canoe were life coming at me. With the inner Prophet in my life, none of it was overwhelming — my boat might be swamped but it wasn't capsized or sunk. But it did need bailing out, and I needed to take charge of that.

During those early months of 2014 I recalled a number of other dreams about renewal and cleaning out. My self-image wasn't changing in any perceptible way, but from my experience around the Guidance for a Better Life retreat center I knew these dreams meant inner change was happening. God was healing me from the inside out.

6
Healing With My Father

At that time my father was succumbing to Alzheimer's Disease. There came a point during his illness where I knew we would never have a heart-to-heart in our physical bodies again; he was having such trouble understanding the simplest things, like where the kitchen sink was. But I knew dreams are a very real place where we could talk. I let God know in prayer I wanted to clear up some old issues with my father before he passed away, and shortly after that I had a dream where we came together to talk. Ahead of time, I had thought he would apologize for his mistakes and I would forgive him, but when we actually met in the dream we both came to the point quickly with a mutual, "Hey, I know I've done things to hurt you, I'm sorry for them, let's move on." In the dream I was my true self and could own up to my own mistakes better than as my waking self. I got the sense that back and forth in various past lives both of us had hurt the other, but all that truly mattered was our deep love for one another. We were not going to count hurts and expect compensation; we were dropping it all. It was the briefest of dreams, but I came away from it knowing we had cleared the air in the deepest sense, and we could leave the past in the past and simply love each other.

This dream was a perfect and timely gift from the inner Prophet. It helped heal an important relationship and that was a gift in itself, but it also made it possible for love to flow in and out of me better, and inner healings ride on love. That is their vehicle.

7

First Rays of Light

An important part of the winter retreats at the retreat center is the Sunday morning HU sing. These are a special opportunity to send love to God, and often students are also blessed with valuable insights. My next retreat was in March, and it was such a relief to follow Del's express instruction to stop trying to contribute to group discussions.

We sang HU for twenty minutes, then sat in rich, peaceful silence for awhile. During this silence several images came to me, all similar. I saw light peeking around obstacles. First a rising sun just peeking above the horizon at dawn as I hiked a craggy mountainside. Then a light shining into a dark room from under a closed door. Other impressions of light shining brightly, strongly from behind a barrier. It felt personal, like the light saw me. I took these images hopefully, God was the Light, and He was not far, there was just a block between us. But doors can be opened and the sun always rises.

In June I was back at the retreat center for a weeklong retreat. Without the usual sense of needing to "perform" for my teacher and the other students, I relaxed into what I knew was a very personal syllabus created specially for me by the inner Prophet. During the week, through a series of guided contemplations, dreams, and alone time I got a chance to see more of the real me, and experienced the beginnings of self-forgiveness. During one experience, I saw myself leaping hand in hand off a cliff with the inner Prophet into a wild ocean, which I found to be actually soft, effervescent, and buoying. This surprised me but in a way it didn't. This water, the life I feared so greatly, was actually my true home. With Prophet at my side, holding my hand, life was a welcome adventure, a joy, fun! I wasn't there yet, but I knew it was possible.

8

Guilt From a Past Life and a Heartfelt Prayer

I mentioned earlier my awareness of a past life where, in my perception, I failed miserably in every way imaginable. Disastrous events affecting many people unfolded for years thanks to my immaturity and carelessness. This was long ago, but I carried massive, paralyzing regret and sorrow from that lifetime all the way into this one. My inability to forgive myself for mistakes made in another life might sound strange — it did to me! I would never do such things in this lifetime and was enormously sorry for having done them in another body. Plus I knew God had forgiven me long ago. Why was I unable to forgive myself, too? At that

June retreat I felt the door to self-forgiveness open just a little.

A special part of the longer retreats at Guidance for a Better Life are the solo mornings. A whole morning alone to contemplate, read, sleep, or hike to a gorgeous spot overlooking the Blue Ridge Mountains. I chose a deeply wooded spot near a babbling stream and found a rock to sit on. There I prayed for help removing barriers between me and God. I asked for help to know who I was. I wrote in my journal:

Dear Lord, dear Father,

Let me now, with your help, pull away the barrier I have placed between us in my mind, perhaps in my heart as well? I have been alone in my thoughts, living in a clutter of fear, worry, and suggestions to and from myself, forgetting your Presence and eagerness to help me. Let me tear up the thought that you disdain my life, this is not true. Let it be settled, finally, that I accept You as my champion and dearest love, let that be a closed matter.

Let me carry away with me, to sustain myself, the everlasting Love I am sensible of in this beautiful woods.

And now I ask, Who am I? Who am I really? Am I gentle? Am I kind? I have seen myself as harsh, even rude. Beneath that is there something softer? Strong but soft, deeply loving and empathic, imaginative and full of fun, brave and warm. The real me resides hidden beneath, joyful and patient, trusting, wise.

Writing these words did something for me I can't quite explain. I believe I really asked God to help me, and declared I was ready to accept His help, and perhaps most importantly, that I was worthy of His help in unearthing the real me.

9

Beginning to Open My Wings

Retreats at Guidance for a Better Life are guided by the inner Prophet, with the syllabus fluid and often surprising, but always perfect for those attending. The last day of that June retreat, what might be called a sharing exercise began, with students one by one taking the small, low stage at the front of the room and testifying about how the love of God was manifesting in their lives. Even the few students like myself who were taking some quiet time were asked to go up and share. When I heard this, I wanted to flee. I wanted to run for the car in the parking lot and hightail it out of there. I was terrified. But I knew this was important. I had to do it, if only to show my gratitude to God for my blessed life. But also to overcome something holding me in a death-grip. When I finally summoned up the courage to get on stage and share my testimony, it was actually great. It was natural and wonderful. I felt all the love of the group shining on me up there on the stage, and at the back of the room Del smiled warmly, joyfully, as he watched his student open her wings and share her voice.

10

Removing Blocks Between Myself and God

The gifts from my retreat were tremendous and I savored them, but as summer waned I almost felt the blocks between God and me even more. It was like clearing away some of the trash in my mind revealed the main obstacles to be removed. I didn't know how to do that though, and had a strong urge to go see a mental health counselor for help with that. I wonder how many counselors not affiliated with a church hear, "I need help removing blocks between me and God," but this lady was completely game. She loved God, too, and understood my desire. We talked for several sessions, and she helped me begin to disentangle from old feelings keeping me from loving myself and others, and ultimately interfering in my relationship with God.

Several weeks into seeing the counselor, I found myself suddenly apologizing to my husband for something I did to him in that distant past life, of which he was also a part. This might sound strange and unnecessary, but for me it was as real and important as needing to seek forgiveness and make amends for badly hurting someone in this lifetime. I sincerely apologized, and he forgave me wholeheartedly. It was something we both needed, and with that hurt between us healed, though it was something we hadn't even been aware of, we were instantly closer and able to love each other more. I know this healing came out of the therapy, which had been urged and organized through the inner Prophet, so ultimately it was a healing from God.

The healings continued to come, subtly in some ways and more dramatically in others.

A healing can begin as an insight, which you could call a healing seed. The seed must be watered to germinate and grow — you must reflect on your God-given insight and deepen your view and understanding of it for it to be of real worth. One important insight I had that fall came to me on a warm, powerful breeze.

It was early October, a warm, rainy night where you leave the door open for the delicious air to come in. I was sitting on the couch when suddenly I heard and felt a strong gust of wind. It was soft but powerful, one of those gusts that inspires you to think, "The winds of change!" A few minutes later, a sudden knowingness came over me that was just like the gust: soft but powerful. I saw that I had never loved myself. I don't know if "never" is correct, but I couldn't recall a time when I did truly love myself. I had never realized it before to this degree, and I had never realized, as I did now, how very important it was. Not loving myself brought to mind the image of a sink with the tap running but the plug out. I love, I am loved, but if I do not love myself something vital is missing and I can never love or be loved or serve God as deeply as I want. I can never be the instrument of God I long to be when I do not love myself. Loving myself is something I must do and something I can do. As this insight came to me, I knew I could love myself. Loving myself would not be hard to do, it was just a matter of opening that channel and including myself as I never had before. Dropping regret over my past was creating the space for that love. It was a strange and wonderful moment, and I was excited about what possibilities might be freed up to come into my consciousness.

Looking back at my dream journal, I see a shift in my dreams after that; I think the insight cleared some space for the real me to start emerging. Change wasn't so obvious in my outer life but dreams, like a three-dimensional ultrasound, can give you a good look at what's going on at a deeper level. The theme of my dreams was "doing what is right for me, taking my own path." In one dream, I was making plans to take a trip to an exotic island in the South Pacific. On the surface the trip looked like a good deal, but as I examined the details I could see it was not. I resisted the sense that I should go through with it to please others, and backed out. This dream showed my typical pattern of following others' lead instead of trusting myself. And it showed me turning, changing, saying no instead of just following along to be pleasing or avoid conflict.

11

Passing of My Father

My father passed away November 1 of that year. What a blessing that we had a chance to meet in a dream and clear the air. What a blessing that I know dreams are real and our dream meeting was real. I know I can sometimes meet him in a dream even though he has passed away, and healings are still possible with deceased loved ones. It made the time of his death and funeral a peaceful one for me, and I was able to share that peace with others. My mother asked me to speak at the funeral, which I agreed to. I found myself looking forward to reading my tribute before the gathering, where in the past I would have been consumed with anxiety about a public speaking situation. The summer retreat's experience of testifying about God's Love was still with me, and I remembered how deeply satisfying it was to share one's love for God and confidence in Him with others.

When I stood up to speak before the large gathering of mourners, I was nervous but not very, just like when I gave my testimony at the summer retreat. Mostly I found myself eager to share about my father and about love. As a professor he had touched many lives and was much loved. I had beautiful quotes to share from many of his past students, and I felt it was important to share them because friends and family had not known him in the same way. After hearing from so many of his students, I could see he was at his very best in the role of teacher. He was often awkward as a parent, friend, or brother, but as a teacher he bloomed, he glowed. He was almost a different creature. This insight was a special gift from God and I wanted those who knew his more cantankerous side to also know, as I had learned, that he was rather like a penguin — awkward in one element, graceful in another. His true self was glorious.

I also wanted the mourners, some of whom I knew doubted the existence of God, Heaven, and a hereafter, to know I was confident in those things. I knew my father was with God now. I knew he would go on, and I would meet him again, even in dreams. This was not the end of him. Quoting the writer Emily Bronte on the subject of death, I stated, "I feel an assurance of the endless and shadowless hereafter — the eternity [he has] entered — where life is boundless in its duration, and love in its sympathy, and joy in its fullness."

After the funeral many people came up to me to thank me for my tribute. A number had no words to describe their reaction it. They just thanked me, and I knew they were responding to the Holy Spirit which had flowed through me. It was such a gift to me to have been used by God to share His Love with those people. And it still surprised me: Not nervous. Actually comfortable, natural. This was another seed God was planting as He helped me find my true self. That image of myself in the little chapel, all eyes on me, quiet enough to hear a pin drop as I listened to and passed on the Word of God. I knew this was the real me, which I still didn't have full access to, but she was in there, under there, somewhere. With patience and in due time, with the guidance of the inner Prophet, we would get to her.

12
Comforting My Mother

Married to him over fifty years, my mother was distraught after my father's death. I didn't realize how horribly she was suffering at first. With my own understanding that we are eternal Souls who reside in bodies which come and go, that we reincarnate over and over with loved ones, that I can see my father occasionally in dreams, that we are still connected closely and aware of each other even if we don't have physical contact, I was peaceful after his death. One evening she opened up about her pain to me. She had lost her father and brother as a little girl, and told me this was worse, frankly. She was in agony, missing him. Part of that agony, she told me, was her deep uncertainty that he still existed. And the idea that he was just gone, completely gone, was awful. I could grasp how awful that must be, and over the following months I helped reassure her that he was still around in some way, that she could talk to him, that he would hear her.

I told Del about this at a January 2015 retreat and he showed me something I'd never thought of: I was the only person my mother could talk to about these things. The only person on the planet. What an honor, what a privilege, to be that for someone. God was entrusting me with the responsibility of teaching her about His Love for His children. This showed me several things: 1) God trusted me, 2) I loved being given that job and wanted to do well at it, 3) we are all special and placed precisely where we are in the world to share Divine love with specific other Souls. These insights built my confidence and also helped clarify who I am and what I want. And perhaps most importantly, built my trust in God — He is looking out for all of us, every one. If you look around with fresh eyes you start seeing the amazing weave of lives and circumstances protecting us, nourishing us, comforting us. Finding myself entrusted with helping my mother on her spiritual journey, I prayed to serve in more ways, to be a vehicle for God in more areas of my life.

13

The Light Grows Stronger

A year after Del had given me the prescription of quiet time, I still felt permission to be quiet at the retreat center but I also felt permission to speak. But my voice felt locked and just imagining speaking up at a retreat filled me with anxiety. I did not feel ready. Still, I wanted to serve. I was, in a sense, my mother's spiritual mentor. What else could I be?

Up at that January retreat, we sang the beautiful HU song again, sending love to God. Nine months previous I had seen a bright light shining from under a door into the dark room where I stood. This time the light was stronger. It had structure and density. It was just dawning on the horizon, but it was strong. The light was magnetically attracted to Earth, and Earth was magnetically attracted to the light. This image was another progress report from the inner Master: I was stronger; my spiritual muscle was denser. My spiritual life was developing a stable structure. There was a long way to go still to operating as my true self, but I was innately drawn to God and God was drawn to me. I was starting to live the words, "Draw nigh to God, and he will draw nigh to you." James 4:8 KJV

A month later at another HU sing, I saw the sun as now fully over the horizon, shining on our faces. It was golden, warm, clear, crisp and vivid. This showed me I was gaining more clarity and progress continued even if I wasn't noticing evidence in my outer life. I knew whatever images and messages I was given during a retreat were from God through His chosen Prophet, and I could trust them. More than I could trust my own mind and its thoughts. I find I can usually differentiate my mind's thoughts from those thoughts within me that come from a Divine place. The thoughts generated in my mind are often fearful or worried, full of judgment and agitation, while the spiritualized thoughts within me, those "God thoughts," are solid, clear and calm. My mind might have been saying I was as screwed up as ever, but my Divine thoughts said otherwise. Things were changing.

14

Awaiting the Harvest

After singing HU, during the beautiful silence that followed, I sat with eyes closed and asked God how to serve. I heard, "Spiritualize the place" as the answer. I thought He meant my workplace, which was a small suite of metalsmiths making custom jewelry where I served as office help. And then I heard, "Joy". And then it was time to open our eyes.

Prophet talked at that retreat about enjoying your life. "One of the greatest tragedies," he said, "is not enjoying every moment God gives us." He continued, "Unhappy is when you're trying to get somewhere you're not. If you're not happy where you are you won't be happy somewhere else." I wrote down these words and wondered about them. I could see I was always wanting to be somewhere else in my spiritual and emotional development; I was unhappy where I was. Being unhappy where you are isn't the same thing as wanting to grow. Wanting to grow is healthy and natural, but being unhappy about where you are now — physical, emotional, spiritual or whatever — stops the flow of love in your life. I realized I needed to be okay with where I was. Be happy with where I was! That didn't mean I wouldn't grow — in fact I was more likely to grow if I embraced myself as I was.

Del's son was at the retreat. He shared from the Bible: "Be patient therefore, brethren, unto the coming of the Lord. Behold, the husbandman waiteth for the precious fruit of the earth, and hath long patience for it, until he receive the early and latter rain." James 5:7 KJV The image of the husbandman (farmer) waiting for the seeds to sprout and emerge from the earth really spoke to me. You do what you can, you do what you know works, and then you must wait. You wait with hope and expectation of good things. And this to me means being happy where you are.

Del told us, "You don't have to straighten yourself out so God wants you. He wants you right now!" Be peaceful with who you are, where you are. God wants you just as you are. Don't wait until you're "in better shape" to get involved. Prophet was getting me ready for what was next, and what was next changed my life in profound and obvious ways; it was a big next step.

15
Sweet Victory

A situation arose in my life, to me a crisis, and I dove in to help; ready or not, it was "all hands on deck." I clung to the inner Prophet for guidance and comfort during a crazy, rocky, months-long ride, and truly had the time of my life, feeling more alive and stronger than I could ever remember. This was being happy where you are and living in the moment, participating in life without waiting to be "ready" first.

I grew up on the campus of the small, rural women's college where my father taught, and also got my bachelor's degree there. It was my beautiful home, and I continued to visit the campus regularly for many years until my father's retirement, when my parents moved away. After that I visited my alma mater rarely, but carried happy memories and appreciation from the twenty-five years I had been so closely associated with it.

In early March 2015 the college suddenly announced it would be closing in August for financial reasons. This came as a complete shock to nearly everyone; something was very wrong with the decision. In my gut I did not feel the college was at the end of its natural life; rather it felt as if the college were being killed, or at least left to die when treatments for its illness were available. Many others felt the same — thousands, in fact. Within a couple days college alumnae were organizing to stop the closure. A nonprofit was established to fight the legal battle and collect donations, and volunteer groups formed to work on needed improvements for various aspects of the college. An independent financial expert determined the college was actually not in such bad shape as to require closing. Our hopes bolstered by this news, we fought harder.

Strangely, the president and board still insisted nothing could be done and continued shutting down operations. It all felt so wrong and so unnecessary. My emotions were high at the thought of my dear childhood home, and the institution to which my father lovingly devoted a third of his life, being perfunctorily dismantled.

I wanted to confirm with the inner Prophet that I was really hearing him, that we were right in trying to save the college. Maybe God had other plans for the campus, students and employees. I started seeing "signs," or what I took as signs, that God wanted us to fight on. I was glad for this, as it was what I truly wanted to do. This was a heart-wrenching time for me, but also a joyful one. I believe this was because I was getting a chance to serve God in my own unique way. I had heard in the previous retreat the words "Spiritualize the place," and this is what God had meant; I was helping bring the Holy Spirit to the fighting arena. In such a struggle people can become very negative, and this shuts down the vital flow of Divine love, creativity, and energy. I was helping keep hearts open and hopeful in small but important ways.

As the days stretched into weeks and the battle raged, I kept my ear tuned to Prophet's voice. Was I becoming too entangled in this? I felt he kept telling me, "Fight on." There were times where he said, "Rest. Step away a little." And then I had his go-ahead to press ahead. I checked with him on how to fight. Mostly this was in the form of trying to uplift and calm and offer hope to the thousands of people I had daily contact with on Facebook. I could sense Prophet saying, "Victory is yours for the earning;" our attitudes and choices would determine the outcome. To this end I made it my business to help foster a cheerful, positive mood among "the troops." I would sometimes post on Facebook lighthearted memes of my own creation to bring a needed laugh; at other times I would share awake dreams or inspiring quotes to refresh hope.

Three weeks into the struggle, it was time for another retreat at Guidance for a Better Life. During the Sunday HU sing, I again saw the sun; I was at a railway station and stepped out from beneath the shade of its roof into full sunlight. God's Love. Fully surrendering, I allowed myself to be vulnerable in bright, healing, cleansing, illuminating light. I found myself holding a mirror or prism in my hand, reflecting God's Light in shades. I knew I was being shown that I was serving in my own style, I was sharing God's Light with the world in my own unique way, but it was definitely still God's Light. I had made it to the place where my journey could pick up speed (the train station), not on the train yet but right there.

I began to have the urge to write a letter to the college's board of trustees, appealing to them to reverse their decision to close. One day, a long letter flowed out of me with ease, and I know Prophet was guiding me as I wrote it. I wrote from the heart, telling the board what I thought had gone wrong with the college and what we were doing to turn it around, and inviting them to join us in the exciting venture of rebuilding. I sent my letter to the board and at the same time it was posted on someone's blog for the public to see. Only receiving three polite thank you notes from board members, it seemed to me they were unmoved to rethink their vote. But something unexpected happened through the blog post; my letter was received with overwhelming enthusiasm by the thousands working to save the college. I received many thank you notes and emails for articulating exactly what was in people's hearts; I was told many times my letter was a great inspiration.

The strong response to my letter confirmed for me that Prophet's voice was audible within it; people were responding to the Holy Spirit. This was my conclusion regarding all my efforts over those four long months: I was being used as a vehicle for God. I loved it, and those around me were fortified by it. I felt so grateful I could serve God simply by being myself in a place I loved. Good things were developing in me: a warrior's spirit and confidence in my voice. The battle was watering seeds in me that had long lain dormant.

In the end the college was saved — an unprecedented event; never before had a college slated to close been saved by its alumni. I thanked God for this! A new president was hired, a new board selected, and it was time to rebuild. The whole place had the feel of clear-eyed, creative, humble workers motivated by love and doing what is right. It feels as if the college is a better place for having gone through this firestorm. It had declined over the years through the complacency of its alumnae and tired, uncreative leadership, but was transforming into something better.

What would this whole episode have looked like without the presence of the inner Prophet? I can scarcely imagine. He bolstered my hope, he guided me in both the big and small questions. Prophet's guidance is God's fresh, Living Word. Without that how could I have functioned effectively during this stressful time? His presence meant this struggle was an amazing adventure. Even if we had not prevailed I would have walked away with priceless gifts.

16

A Green Light to Serve

I was different after this small-scale war. I saw myself in a new light. I saw myself more as others did. I was a leader. I was a warrior. I was a brilliant writer. I was a comedian. I had to admit these things were true. These were my gifts. I was stronger, and so was my relationship with God through His Prophet. I was so humbled and grateful that God cared about my college — or cared about how much I loved my college — that He would support our efforts.

Old abilities were uncovered in me, restoring a confidence unknown in this lifetime. As much as I had changed, however, that confidence did not extend to being a student at Guidance for a Better Life. There I was still afraid to open my mouth for fear garbage would spill out. The emergency I had found myself in, the imminent closing of my college, had been the perfect medium to show up as my true self. With things returning to normal, I didn't have something to draw me out. Yet I had seen a glimpse of the real me and I trusted she would emerge more and more.

In late June, as the college drama was coming to a close, I attended another weeklong retreat at Guidance for a Better Life. The first night, we turned over the upcoming week to the inner Prophet. We prayed, asking him to guide our week, surrendering how it would look and what we would learn, and committing to helping each other get the most out of our time. During that opening surrender, I saw in my inner vision a number of green lights. They were brightly lit, infused with gold. I immediately saw this as the proverbial "green light." God was giving me the green light to go forward and serve my way in my world. I accepted that I must be ready, even if I didn't necessarily feel ready. It wasn't just one green light, it was a whole bank of them. God was saying, "You're ready in all areas." After that I saw a very bright golden light, the Light of God, and myself walking hand in hand with Prophet toward that glorious light.

17
No More Digging Up the Past

During the week I dreamed about a friend from college. She was trying to lift up some old, heavy stone steps to reveal worms underneath and clear them out. Prophet was there and kept pushing the stones back down into their original places so she couldn't clear out the worms. I knew from experience that the people in our dreams are usually aspects of ourself, and this I trusted was no exception. The dream was showing me Prophet didn't want me to dig up my past in order to heal it. It's not that I shouldn't deal with it, but I shouldn't deal with it in that way: alone, digging into the heavy, dank dirt of it. Removing the stones was actually removing steps, steps we need to climb to get where we're going. Healing comes from shining God's Light on our past, not from dwelling on it in our minds.

This was reinforced by something Del said at one point during the week, "Don't keep going back to past mistakes. Start seeing yourself as you are now and move forward." This was underlined by words I heard alone in the woods: "No more. Enough." It was time to stop beating myself up for past mistakes in this lifetime and others. Wherever. No more.

In an inner conversation with Prophet that week, he told me, "I love you and I want to see you free." I asked him how I could do that, and he explained that while I had excellent instincts I was not putting the period on the sentence, "I love myself." That kept it from coming together completely. It kept me from fully engaging, trusting myself, and trusting I was hearing Prophet correctly. To say, "I love myself. Period." is vastly different from trailing off with no period. I love myself, dot dot dot. All the "buts" reside in those dots. All the reasons you still don't think you're fully loveable, or you don't deserve to be loved as much as others. I still hadn't fully closed the stopper on my "love sink."

An inner conversation I had with a beautiful spiritual being during one contemplation that week really helped me see how God loves me. And if God loves me so much, shouldn't I love myself? She told me each of us, each and every Soul, is totally unique and amazing to God. Including me. Amazing to God. That really struck me; we are each special to Him, every person, none more or less so than another. And He loves each of us with awe. Can you imagine? God is in awe of His creation, you. He is not unamazed even though He has created so much and so many. I trusted this spiritual being and anything she would claim about the ways of God. If I could truly accept what she said as true, how could I continue to see myself as not good enough?

18

The Shorts of Truth

I spent the rest of the summer in some sort of germination state. Certainly all the experience with my college from the previous spring, coupled with the encouraging prompts I had received from God through His Prophet were working inside me. In my outer form, however, I found myself at the heaviest I had ever been. Somehow I had slipped into eating ice cream every evening. Ordering Cokes whenever we went out. And never exercising. My sister had taken me shopping in July and introduced me to maxi dresses — full-length dresses with a flattering cut which hide all kinds of figure flaws beneath their flowing drape. When I did put on a pair of shorts I noticed they were tighter, with some of them not as comfortable as they used to be. Now in my mid-forties, I'd accepted I was up a couple of sizes, but then came the "Shorts of Truth."

I had a pair of shorts, which had always fit, always always. They're plain old cargo shorts I've had for something like five years. They always fit and they always look fine. One day, well into the season of maxi dresses, I put them on and probably gasped out loud. What had happened? I had a lightning-fast thought that someone mischievous had switched out my shorts with another, identical pair, just way tighter. As I stared at myself in the mirror the truth sank in. I had put on a lot of weight. These shorts which had always fit were actually skin-tight. It was a shock. I knew it hadn't all happened during the summer of the maxi dress, but had been creeping on for years and escalated in the last couple of months.

After my initial shock, I found myself quite calm. I think this calm demonstrates the inner transformation that had been building over the previous year and a half. I turned straight to the inner Prophet and said, "What do we do about this?" Not beating myself up, not daunted by the task of losing a significant amount of weight. I knew with the guidance of Prophet this would not be overwhelming. I also carried around this sense of confidence since the college had been saved. If we could do that, well, anything was possible.

Del often talks about the principle of not looking at the whole task you have before you but just the first step or two. That way it doesn't feel overwhelming and scare you off the whole thing. I didn't go to "I need to go on a diet" which would be daunting and doomed to failure in the long term, but instead I said, "I need to stop eating sugar." I decided I could have sugar, but only if I put a dollar into a jar for a charity each time. This little game kept my sugar eating under control without being a big red "no" before me. The inner Prophet also suggested I start taking daily walks. So I wasn't starving or working out like a maniac, just taking small steps. The last suggestion I received from the Divine was to start a Facebook page for alumnae from my college also interested in getting fit.

Losing weight in this way was actually fun and easy. It only took a few days to overcome my cravings for sugar, and staying away from it quickly became easy. It was fall, and my daughter and I would head down to a local walking trail with the dogs after school, where we all spent a pleasant couple hours moving in nature. Following Del's principle of adding a step at a time to the task, I found myself naturally wanting to take it further — adding in a fun Indian dance workout DVD which had been lying around for years collecting dust, a little jump rope, and some yoga workouts with a friendly YouTube instructor. I started meeting a friend some mornings to walk our dogs together before we needed to get our kids off to school. Sometimes I ran a little during my walks. I made an effort every day but never got extreme. Looking back at it, I can see that my approach to getting fit was the same as my "spiritual fitness program;" I made slow, steady progress listening to the inner Prophet, following my own path, putting in real effort but not pushing myself too hard. Twenty pounds melted off this way, much to my delight.

19

Changing Outside and In

During this time I still had self-doubt. I wasn't doing anything that looked spiritual to me. How was helping save a college and focusing on my health and fitness spiritual? In my little box of perspective, these were not spiritual things. I compared myself with other students at Guidance for a Better Life and judged their lives to be more spiritual than mine. I supposed they thought about God more than I do, and did things that truly could be called service to Him. At the same time, just as during the season of saving the college, I felt Prophet's support in what I was doing. I felt he'd helped me design the fitness program and in a way I was doing something to serve God; I was getting happy and healthy and reflecting joy everywhere I went. The fitness Facebook group quickly grew to about three hundred people, many of whom would tell me they appreciated my cheerful, uplifting posts and credited the group with helping them get healthier. I physically felt better in my own skin, and I wondered: Could getting comfortable in your own skin also come from the outside in? Could losing weight and gaining muscle and physical energy also be losing spiritual baggage and gaining spiritual strength? I couldn't shake the feeling that my physical health program was an important component of God's overall program for me to find my true self. And I had the feeling my inner condition was reflected in my outer condition. I was getting affirmation that I really was changing on the inside.

Another important thing I found as I started exercising regularly was that it helped so much with my moods. If I was feeling anxious or down I'd go and exercise and feel better afterwards. Then I heard exercise had been scientifically proven as more effective for many mood issues than medication. I also learned during that time yoga is proven to help with developing a sense of peace and self-confidence. The Divine sent me these pieces of information to give me confidence in what I was doing. It wanted me to know I was on the right path, even though it might not appear spiritual to me.

20
Self-Reverence

At a Guidance for a Better Life retreat in October 2015 the term "self-reverence" came up: acknowledging and respecting our own divinity as creations of God. It's treating this creation as sacred. It is right and proper to have reverence for ourselves. I realized I was showing more self-reverence in taking better care of the body God gave me. This is my wondrous, miraculous vehicle God made especially for me, and it feels good to think of it that way and try to care for it better. I wonder if taking better care of one's body is often a part of inner change.

During that October retreat I had two dreams. In one of them, I had a cotton tote bag. I was comparing it to a fancy, patent leather one I thought seemed the better bag, but I had a feeling the cotton one was actually better. It was so practical because it was strong and washable too. In the other dream I remembered I had a necklace with a painted wooden bead on it. At first I thought I should try to get a better bead, one with a genuine gemstone instead. But then I realized the wooden one had some kind of receiver in it, and I knew I could receive information from God via that bead. So even though the outside was humble it was more useful to me. The tote bag and the bead both reinforced I was making choices that worked for me; they might not look right to me, or even to others, but they were helping me with what I wanted to do and to get where I wanted to go.

These dreams fit in with one of the discourses from that October retreat about perfection. Prophet taught us that we are actually not capable of saying what "perfection" is. Sometimes we serve God best because of our imperfections — they are what makes our service perfect! All we need to do is listen and pass on God's Word to the best of our abilities. Prophet said, "The best way to show reverence is to stay the course, walk the walk, keep your focus, and don't give up on yourself." As unorthodox as I felt my path was, hearing this made me feel I was actually listening to God and following His path.

At the very end of the weekend, Del approached me and invited me to a weeklong retreat to be held in April known as Spirit Week. Students at Guidance for a Better Life are only invited to attend these every few years. They are small — about eight students — and a wonderful opportunity to grow. The prescribed quiet time was past, but I was still not comfortable speaking and contributing in class. He said maybe Spirit Week was exactly what I needed and I agreed. I knew I was making progress, but the extra face-to-face time with the Prophet would certainly push it, whatever it was, over the crest of the mountain I had been ascending for nearly two years. I was grateful and excited for the week, about six months away.

21

I Am Worthy of God's Love

A month later I was back for another weekend retreat. We were once again singing HU together, and I tried to send God as much love as I could in each HU I sang. I visualized my Hus going out to God, and God accepting them. And then it struck me: Part of God is also within me. I saw the golden Light of God within me, and it was undeniable that His Spirit resides within me. I am worthy, by definition of His being there. I was totally bowled over by a profound sense of relief and gratitude. Words fail to convey how enormous this insight was, but it floored me. I found myself weeping (silently so as not to disturb the others), and unable to sing HU for a couple minutes, I was so overcome. In the silence after the HU, I took a deep breath. It was the first breath I could remember ever enjoying being mine. I rejoiced in the possibility of being truly comfortable and happy to be in my own skin. This felt like a massive healing, one I must take care to nurture. Healings must be remembered and contemplated upon to take root in your life. A part of God lives inside me, and I am worthy. To know this, not just think this, was deeply transformative.

22
Forgiving My Past

Back for another retreat in January 2016, another huge piece fell into place. Prophet told me that when he looked at me he saw an emotionally tortured person, self-tortured for thousands of years. He said he saw a contorted agony on my face, beneath the smile; he had always seen it. This was a crystallizing moment for me, and actually a huge relief to hear this, because I saw it too. It was like finally finding the doctor who is able to diagnose your symptoms and you know you're going to get the treatment that will work. Hearing him say it made me feel something could be done; I could finally be free of this thing I'd been carrying. It seemed this was the key to everything that had baffled and frustrated me about myself. Why hadn't Prophet told me this before? It simply wasn't time. Now it was. God's timing is always perfect.

We sang HU together and as we did I felt God drawing nigh to me; I knew it was because I had drawn nigh to Him. I had a peaceful knowingness that He would help me pinpoint the ages-old source of this agony and heal it because I had dropped resistance to Divine truth. The room became very bright in my inner vision as the healing Light of God was upon me.

When Del mentioned a self-torture in me thousands of years old, I immediately suspected it was that lifetime where I had failed so abysmally as a wife, mother, and servant to God. I was still hanging onto the shame of it, part of me refusing to forgive myself, as much as I tried. When we do something really bad, we often decide the best response is to hold deep shame for our actions. This, we feel, is the best way to express our contrition for our sins. Forgiving ourselves might be excusing behavior that hurt others.

I could see the shadow that lifetime cast over this one, making me continue to lack reverence for myself. I was not able to accept God's Love the way I wanted to. I still struggled to be myself, to speak and act without paralyzing self-consciousness, to live life fully. My ability to feel and receive comfort still felt numbed or coated in a plastic barrier so I didn't really experience it. While I had experienced a lot of moments being myself, enough so I knew what it felt like, it was so often out of reach.

I had tried to forgive myself, knowing that was important. I knew God had forgiven me, and my husband, also incarnated in that lifetime, had forgiven me too. But now I knew I simply hadn't done it. Now I knew the only way to live this lifetime fully was to forgive myself for acts in that lifetime still living strongly within me. But I didn't seem to be able to make myself.

I decided to go back to the therapist I had seen about a year and a half previously. Or more accurately, I could say I felt the inner Prophet suggesting I talk to her to get past this. I didn't bring this up directly with her, but rather we worked on how I could calm myself when anxiety was triggered. Come back to a place of clarity and peace instead of locking up or having my thoughts race unproductively.

Along the way she shared with me some research on shame by a woman named Brené Brown. It hit me like a thunderbolt. Here was the other side of carrying shame: Shame never, ever, creates anything positive; it is never the catalyst for real and lasting change. In fact, shame is responsible, according to extensive research, for a host of self-destructive behaviors. This is simply a fact. Shame is different from guilt. Guilt can actually create something positive — guilt is seeing your responsibility for a mistake. Guilt says, "I did something wrong" while shame says, "I am something wrong." Guilt leaves the door open for fixing and improving things; shame closes it.

I took this a step further: Holding shame does nothing to bring you closer to God. You cannot serve fully; you cannot love God fully. You squander your Divine gifts when you insist you are not worthy. When you hold shame you are not loving yourself. You are not letting the Light of God shine on you. You are, in truth, disagreeing with God. You are telling God, "No. I am not worthy." Imagine that. Telling God He is wrong about you. Others' mistakes might be forgivable, but not yours. Whoa, that really hit me. In a good way. I decided on the spot I had no business hanging onto shame. It cut me off from God and it was also me telling Him, He was wrong and I was right. Nothing could have convinced me quicker to let go of beating myself up for past failings!

My mistakes are forgivable. All mistakes are forgivable. I cannot say there was a moment I remember forgiving myself, where I said, "I forgive you, Joan," and felt it sink in, leaving me transformed. It was more like a cloud evaporating. Quietly, unnoticed, except you realize it's brighter after a little while. I noticed one day it was easier to look at my own face in the mirror. I looked, and my eyes were looking straight back, clear and open. It's hard to explain. But something was gone that in the past made the experience of looking at my face sad and painful.

Attending another weekend retreat in March, Del noticed the difference too. "I don't see that tortured face anymore," he observed. During our Sunday HU, my primary sense was confidence and trust in God, closeness and warmth. The HU felt active and purposeful. I felt a nurturing, solid relaxedness and peace as we were bathed in God's golden Light.

23

Attached to My Story

As the April Spirit Week approached, I continued to see my counselor to help me disarm automatic responses that would get triggered by anything appearing stressful in my mind. At one point, my counselor looked at me and said something like, "I submit to you that you're too attached to your story." The wording was sort of unusual and formal and felt like a deep appeal to please move past events that were over but still impeding my progress. Her statement drifted around in my thoughts for days. I wondered about it.

A few days before the retreat I was standing in our kitchen and suddenly her words seemed to manifest into something tangible, almost physical. I saw my father handing me an object, something brass. It was sort of like one of those intricate gadgets you see in turn of the century sci-fi movies, a heavy, capsule-shaped mechanism. There he was handing it to me, my father trying to pass onto me something he thought I should have — my inheritance. I paused a moment, then politely, firmly, lovingly declined it. It was not something I wanted. As much as he believed it was a helpful device for me to have, no, I would not take it. The vision faded away. We sat down as a family to watch a movie then, but part of me was still in this experience. My choice not to accept the "story," those limiting beliefs about who I am and what I can be, broadened before me. I saw expanses of possibility. I saw I truly could do anything I wanted to. I was limitless. The endless worlds and love of God were all around me to explore, to move about in freely.

The capsule of behaviors and beliefs my father was handing me were not just his, or even those passed down to him. It symbolized all the beliefs keeping me earthbound, those I gathered in this life as well as in others. By the Grace of God, I received in the kitchen that evening a big download of clarity allowing me to really see this. It was the story separating me from God and from being my true self. With this clarity, I simply have to make a choice, and I choose not to accept the story.

24

Clarity at Spirit Week

Our first day up at Spirit Week, Del asked us to each find a place to sit somewhere outside the small cabin where retreats were held and contemplate on what we wanted help with that week. I found a comfortable, sunny seat among some leafless, early-April trees and tried to settle in. But I was anxious. I could see my lifelong mechanisms still at work: I was worried I wouldn't be perfect during our retreat. I wanted so badly to truly be free of this need to impress, and prayed to God the week would help me finally be comfortable and relaxed in my own skin. I also prayed for help loving myself just as I am. I wanted to trust my voice. I had worked so hard to have these things but they still felt just beyond my grasp.

After Del called us back to the cabin, I shared my list of goals with him and the group. He suggested a major part of my week would be about gaining clarity. In gaining clarity I would gain strength. It is fatiguing to be unclear, he said. I could gain clarity about when my brain was saying something, and when my thoughts were divinely inspired. The room seemed to get very still and warm as he spoke. It was filled with golden, afternoon sunshine streaming through the window, but I know it was more than physical light I was perceiving. Something special was happening. I would say I was being bathed in God's healing Light, God's Grace. Sometimes God just takes something away you don't need anymore.

Over this week in the physical presence of the living Prophet I saw with more and more clarity. About myself, and even about specific things I was dealing with in my life. It was like my brain was able to operate so much better, like it was upgraded. I had decoding manuals all around me for whatever I needed to look at. I felt a growing confidence and strength throughout my being, and had a number of vivid dreams which built my understanding. It was like all the work I had done over the past couple of years started coming together that week in that cabin. All the insights I had been given were falling into place and helping me feel good and natural in my skin.

And then I had a special dream I'll always remember. I was in a large, fancy hotel, the kind with a spacious, high-ceilinged lobby and brass chandeliers, and I was riding a donkey or a mule with no bridle or saddle all over the pristine carpets. There were other donkeys and mules in the lobby. The one I was riding was attracted to the others, almost magnetically. It was strong and hearty, and would basically take off running toward one of its friends while I just hung on with no real means of guiding it. It had enormous energy and joy. I was thinking "donkeys shouldn't be in places like this," but then it wasn't doing any harm. It was just seeking out its kind. I shared the dream with Del and he just seemed to beam. "Well, this was an easy dream to interpret," he said with a smile. The donkey or mule I was riding is the true me. I'm joyful and energetic, with a good heart. My mind might not think I'm spiritual enough — donkeys and mules don't belong in five-star hotels — but my spirituality doesn't have to look like anyone else's. It isn't anyone else's. It's my unique style. It's my unique skin, created with love by God. I am that happy, strong donkey plunging around in my life. I'm not doing anything other than trying to give and receive love. I bring joy when I am myself, my authentic self, even if I'm kind of like a barn animal running around on fine carpet. It makes God happy, and it makes me happy.

I kept returning to that dream as the days passed. I was so grateful to God that He not only accepts but appreciates my happy donkey self. Del told me my focus should be on just accepting love, enjoying my path, and appreciating the daily abundance that came with it. There was no need to do anything big and fancy. I felt such freedom to just have fun in life, serving God in this way. Many times that week, from across the room Del would frame me in his vision with his hands, stating emphatically, "This is the real you!" when I expressed myself in bold, clear words. It echoes and echoes, that vision of Prophet declaring, "This is the real you!"

25

Checkmate

I recently heard Del tell another student, "You've checkmated yourself. In a good way." Those who know chess know this means you can't make a single move that will save your king. The game is over. I loved the image. I too had checkmated myself; over the past two plus years I had put myself in a position where I finally had to see myself as God does. I came face to face with the fact that "This is the real you!" It was showed to me in such obvious ways. By the physical Prophet, by the inner Prophet. I can see it, and it's undeniable. I cannot turn away from it or explain it away. Checkmate. In a good way.

So now what? Having reached this higher ground, I feel so different, but I still know ground can be lost; just as with physical fitness, spiritual fitness can be lost. Just as with your physical health, it requires maintaining good habits — nothing need be earthshaking about them, just common sense good habits.

Ask for help from God maintaining — and continuing to build — the new self image. Where you've got to isn't the end, you keep evolving. It makes you stronger to ask for help. It builds your humility. Use your creativity; keep creatively revisiting the realization of who you are, replacing the old image. Go back to relive those wonderful moments where you experienced a particular healing. That old image can come up during times of stress or fatigue so do not be surprised. Keep doing the things that got you to the good place, but give yourself a break and don't panic if you do not feel like the true you every single day. Just know you can get back to it and do what works to feel like yourself again. Ask for God's help!

We were made to give and receive Divine love, each in our unique way. Much freer from my self-limiting views, I look around and see new ways to give and receive love in my life. I have the energy and the confidence to dream of an abundant future and work toward creating it. My sphere of living is finally expanding rather than contracting, bringing love and joy to all it encompasses. I call this a miracle. Thank you God, thank you Prophet.

26
Comfortable In My Own Skin

Being comfortable in your own skin. We've all heard the expression. I think we all instinctively like the sound of it. Many of us are not comfortable in our own skin and don't know how to get there, although we know it's where we want to get. I want to tell you in closing: you can do it. And it's worth it. Being comfortable in your own skin is glorious. Your own skin is a gift from God to you. Just to be in it, wholly, is wondrous. It was made for you — with love — by the Almighty. You can get there. As Prophet says, "Never give up on yourself." God won't.

I hope my story helps you see the path you take doesn't have to fit your idea of perfection to be the right one. And your true self might not look "spiritually correct" to you. I had no idea my path would take me through saving a college and weight loss. I had no idea the real me would be a rough and ready donkey. And yet, deep down I must have known because I embraced these things with conviction as they came to me. Trust yourself and the Divine wisdom deep within as you follow the exciting path to your true self.

Guidance for a Better Life
Our Story

My Father's Journey

Prophet Del Hall III

God always has a living Prophet on Earth to teach His Ways and accomplish His will. My father, Del Hall III, is currently God's true Prophet fully raised up and ordained by God Himself. He was not always a Prophet, nor did he even know what a Prophet was, but God had a plan for him like He has for all of His children. Over many years through many life experiences, God had begun to prepare my father for his future assignment, mostly unbeknownst to him. Everything he experienced in his life from the joys to the sadness helped prepare him for his future role as Prophet.

My dad grew up in California and was a decent student but a better athlete. He received an appointment to the United States Naval Academy in Annapolis, Maryland where he later met my mother. They were married two days after he graduated and received his commission as an officer. After a short tour on a Navy ship deployed to Vietnam, he went to flight training school and became a Navy fighter pilot. While attending flight school in Pensacola, Florida he also earned a Master of Science Degree and had the first of his three children, a son. After flight school he was stationed in a fighter squadron on the East Coast, where he and my mom began investing in real estate, adding to their family with the birth of two daughters. Following this tour of duty he was assigned as a jet flight instructor in Texas, after which, his time in the Navy was finished. He was a natural pilot and loved his time in the sky, but it was time to move on.

So far in life he had no real concern for, or even thought much about God, religion, or spiritual matters in general. He lived life fully. He raised his family. He traveled. He invested and became an entrepreneur starting and growing highly successful businesses in diverse fields ranging from real estate to aerospace consulting. Years before however, a seed had been planted when God's eternal teachings were introduced to him in his late teens, and while it did not show outwardly, the truth in these teachings spoke to his heart. My dad might not have been giving much thought about God up to this point in his life, but God was definitely thinking about him and the future He had planned for him. Like an acorn destined to become a mighty oak, the seed that lay dormant in his heart would someday be stirred to life. Through all his life experiences, both "good" and "bad," God would be preparing him for his future role as His Prophet.

When God decided it was time, He called my dad to Him. He did this by shutting down the world of financial security my dad had built. Over a period of two years all of his businesses were wound down and dissolved. What seemed like security turned out to be an illusion. Financial success had not provided true security. He now had failed businesses and a failing marriage and was trying to fix things without God's help, principles, or guidance. As painful as this time in his life was, it was yet another step towards the glorious life of service awaiting my father. God was removing him from the world my dad had created and furthering him along his path to his future role as Prophet.

After his marriage ended and his businesses wound down, he started fresh by going out west to give flying lessons near Lake Mead, Nevada. While living in Nevada my dad was reintroduced to the eternal teachings of God he first learned of as a teenager twenty-three years earlier, and though they resonated with him at the time, his priorities were different back then. Now, his serious training could begin. He started having very clear experiences with the Holy Spirit and noticed there was a familiarity with these teachings and experiences. He embraced the long hours of instruction, which often lasted until sunrise, and was receptive to the personal spiritual experiences he was given. This began an intense period of study and desire for spiritual truth that continues to this day. Some of his most profound and meaningful experiences during this time were with past Prophets of old. They came to him spiritually in contemplations and dreams. He learned of their roles in history and how they were raised up and ordained by God directly. He began to realize they were training him but was not clear why. A few times his experiences led him to believe he was in training to be a future Prophet. However, that revelation made no sense to him because he felt he was an imperfect person who made mistakes and had failures. He thought of the past and current Prophets of God as perfected Souls, not imperfect like he felt he was. Why would God choose him for such a role? He did not feel qualified.

Besides being introduced to God's teachings while he was out west, my father was blessed to meet his current wife Lynne. Returning to the East Coast, my father and Lynne moved into a small cabin on land he had acquired before his businesses shut down. This was a major change in his life, but it felt deeply right within him. He began to remember a desire to live like this as a child; from early childhood my dad found clarity and peace in nature. He had forgotten about this until now, but God had not and made this dream a reality. In addition to being their home, these beautiful, three-hundred-plus acres of land in the Blue Ridge Mountains would eventually become the location for the Guidance for a Better Life retreat center. The perfection of my father's experiences from earlier in his life in real estate, providing the land for his next step in life, speaks to the perfection of God's plan. One of many many examples I could list.

For many years my dad took wilderness skills courses around the country. He specialized in the study of wild edible and medicinal plants, tracking, and awareness skills, and authored articles for publication. Inspired to help folks feel more comfortable in the outdoors, my dad and Lynne began the Nature Awareness School in 1990.

Classes were focused on teaching awareness and the primitive living skills needed to enjoy the woods and survive in them if necessary. An amazing thing happened within those first few years though; students began to experience aspects of God in very personal and dramatic ways. Somewhat like my dad's experience out west, they found that stepping away from their daily routine and the hustle of life, if even for a few days, created space for Spirit to do Its work. Whether they were enjoying the beauty of the Virginia wilderness and tranquility of the school grounds or relaxing by the pond, he found students' hearts opened, and they became more receptive to the Divine Hand that is always reaching out to Its children. More and more the discourse during wilderness classes shifted to the meanings of dreams, personal growth, finding balance in life, and experiences the students were having with the Voice of God in Its many forms. An increase of spiritual retreats was offered to fulfill the demand and over time became the predominant class offerings; the wilderness survival skills classes eventually fading away completely. The name "Nature Awareness School" seemed to be less fitting for what was actually being taught now and in February 2019 my father changed the name of the retreat center to Guidance for a Better Life.

Throughout this time my father's training and spiritual study continued. My father reached mastership and was ordained by God on July 7, 1999 but he was still not yet Prophet, more was required. On October 22, 2012, twenty-five years since his full-time intensive training had begun, God ordained him as His chosen Prophet, and He has continued to raise him up further since. God works through my father in very direct and beneficial ways for his students. Hundreds and hundreds of students for more than thirty years have received God's eternal teachings through my father's instruction and mentoring. They have had personal experiences with the Divine which have transformed and greatly blessed their lives. My father's greatest joy is being used by God as a servant to share God's ways and truths with thirsty Souls and hungry seekers. In addition to mountaintop retreats, my father continues to spread God's ways and teachings that so greatly blessed his life and the lives of his loved ones in many ways, including his books and videos.

Maybe you are at a turning point in your life and looking for direction. Maybe you have a knowing there is more to life but not sure what that might be or how to find it. Or, maybe you are simply drawn to what you read and hear in our stories. God speaks to our hearts and calls each of us in many different ways. Like my father's journey demonstrates, it doesn't matter where you started or the twists, turns, or seeming dead-ends your life has taken; God wants us to know Him more fully, and for us to know our purpose within His creation. He wants us to experience His Love regardless of our religious path or lack thereof. He always has a living Prophet here on Earth to help us accomplish His desire for us — to show us the way home to Him and to experience more abundance in our lives while we are still living here on Earth. God's Prophet today is my father, Del Hall III. You have the opportunity to grow spiritually through God's teachings which Prophet shares. His guidance for a better life is available for you — please accept it.

Written by Del Hall IV

My Son, Del Hall IV

My son, Del Hall IV, joined Guidance for a Better Life as an instructor after fifteen years of in-class training with me, his father. He helped develop the five-step Keys to Spiritual Freedom Study Program and

Del Hall IV

facilitates the first two courses in the program: Step One "Tools to Recognize Divine Guidance" and Step Two "Understanding Divine Guidance." Del also teaches people about the rich history of dream study and how to better recall their own dreams during the Dream Study Workshops, which he hosts around the country. He is qualified to step in and facilitate any of my retreats should the need arise.

Del authored the book *God is in the Garden*, a priceless book of wisdom in the form of parables. Through stories of everyday events of life on the mountain Del shares profound insights into the nature of God and life that are infused with his natural humor and unique perspective.

Del is also Vice President of Marketing and helps with everything required to get the "good news" from Guidance for a Better Life out to hungry seekers: everything from book publishing, blogging, and posting on social media outlets. He is co-author and book cover designer for many of our, thus far, twenty published books.

My son loves the opportunity to work on creative projects for Guidance for a Better Life. From a very early age he has been an artist and loved creating artwork in multiple mediums. He was accepted into gifted art programs in Virginia Beach, Virginia and then after high school graduation he attended the School of the Museum of Fine Arts in Boston. He is now a nationally exhibited artist and his *Paintings of the Light and Sound of God* are in over two hundred public and private collections. One of the greatest joys of the painting process for Del is using his paintings as an opportunity to share with others the inspiration behind them, God's Love and his experiences with the Light and Sound of God, the Holy Spirit, in contemplation and in waking life.

Del lives on the retreat center property in the Blue Ridge Mountains of Virginia with his wife where they raised and homeschooled my three grandchildren. Recently he helped me with an extensive renovation and update for the three hand-built log cabins on retreat center property originally used for advanced spiritual retreats. He loves woodworking, tending to his vegetable garden, pruning his fruit trees, and helping maintain the beautiful three-hundred acres of retreat center property for students to enjoy. There is always something that needs attention on the land and Del is always up to the challenge. He loves to travel and spends his free time enjoying this beautiful country with his family in their RV.

My son has had multiple brain surgeries starting when he was seventeen years old for a recurring brain tumor. He credits God for surviving and thriving all this time when most with his condition do not. He looks to the sunrise every day with gratitude for yet another chance at life. With that chance he desires to help me share the love and teachings of God that have so blessed our lives. I pray to God daily thanking Him for my son's good health.

Written by Prophet Del Hall

What is the Role of God's Prophet?

An introductory understanding of God's handpicked and Divinely trained Prophet is necessary to fully benefit from reading this book. God ALWAYS has a living Prophet of His choice on Earth. He has a physical body with a limited number of students, but the inner spiritual side of Prophet is limitless. Spiritually he can help countless numbers of Souls all over the world, no matter what religion or path they are on — even if that is no path at all. He teaches the ways of God and shares the Light and Sound of God. He delivers the living Word of God. Prophet can teach you physically as well as through dreams, and he can lift you into the Heavens of God. He offers protection, peace, teachings, guidance, healing, and love.

Each of God's Prophets throughout history has a unique mission. One may only have a few students with the sole intent to keep God's teachings and truth alive. God may use another to change the course of history. God's Prophets are usually trained by both the current and former Prophets. The Prophet is tested and trained over a very long period of time. The earlier Prophets are physically gone but teach the new Prophet in the inner spiritual worlds. This serves two main purposes: the trainee becomes very adept at spiritual travel and gains wisdom from those in whose shoes he will someday walk. This is vital training because the Prophet is the one who must safely prepare and then take his students into the Heavens and back.

There are many levels of Heaven, also called planes or mansions. Saint Paul once claimed to know a man who went to the third Heaven. Actually it was Paul himself that went, but the pearl is, if there is a third Heaven, it presumes a first and second Heaven also exist. The first Heaven is often referred to as the Astral plane. Even on just that one plane of existence there are over one hundred sub-planes. This Heaven is where most people go after passing, unless they receive training while still here in their physical body. Without a guide who is trained properly in the ways of God a student could misunderstand the intended lesson and become confused as to what is truth. The inner worlds are enormous compared to the physical worlds. They are very real and can be explored safely when guided by God's Prophet.

Part of my mission is to share more of what is spiritually possible for you as a child of God. Few Souls know or understand that God's Prophet can safely guide God's children, while still alive physically, to their Heavenly Home. Taking a child of God into the Heavens is not the job of clergy. Clergy have a responsibility to pass on the teaching of their religion exactly as they were taught, not to add additional concepts or possibilities. If every clergy member taught their own personal belief system no religion could survive for long. Then the beautiful teachings of an earlier Prophet of God would be lost. Clergy can be creative in finding interesting and uplifting ways to share their teachings, but their job is to keep their religion intact. However, God sends His Prophets to build on the teachings of His past Prophets, to share God's Light and Love, to teach His language, and to guide Souls to their Heavenly Home.

There is ALWAYS MORE when it comes to God's teachings and truth. No one Prophet can teach ALL of God's ways. It may be that the audience of a particular time in history cannot absorb more wisdom. It could be due to a Prophet's limited time to teach and limited time in a physical body on Earth. Ultimately, it is that there is ALWAYS MORE! Each of God's Prophets brings additional teachings and opportunities for ways to draw closer to God, building on the work and teachings of former Prophets. That is one reason why Prophets of the past ask God to send another; to comfort, teach, and continue to help God's children grow into greater abundance. Former Prophets continue to have great love for God's children and want to see them continue to grow in accepting more of God's Love. One never needs to stop loving or accepting help from a past Prophet in order to grow with the help of the current Prophet. All true Prophets of God work together and help one another to do God's work.

All the testimonies in this book were written by students at the Guidance for a Better Life retreat center. It is here that the nature of God, the Holy Spirit, and the nature of Soul are EXPERIENCED under the guidance of a true living Prophet of God. Guidance for a Better Life is NOT a religion, it is a retreat center. God and His Prophet are NOT disparaging of any religion of love. However, the more a path defines itself with its teachings, dogma, or tenets, the more "walls" it inadvertently creates between the seeker and God. Sometimes it even puts God into a smaller box. God does not fit in any box. Prophet is for all Souls and is purposely not officially aligned with any path, but shows respect to all.

YOU can truly have an ABUNDANT LIFE through a personal and loving relationship with God, the Holy Spirit, and God's ordained Prophet. This is my primary message to you. Having a closer relationship with the Divine requires understanding the "Language of the Divine." God expresses His Love to us, His children, in many different and sometimes very subtle ways. Often His

Love goes unrecognized and unaccepted because His language is not well known. The testimonies in this book have shown you some of the ways in which God expresses His Love. It is my hope that in reading this book, you have begun to learn more of the "Language of the Divine." The stories spanned from very subtle Divine guidance to profound examples of experiencing God up close and very personal. After reading this book I hope you now know your relationship with God has the potential to be more profound, more personal, and more loving than any organized religion on Earth currently teaches.

If you wish to develop a relationship with God's Prophet, seek the inner side of Prophet, for he is spiritually already with you. Few are able to meet the current physical incarnation and most people do not need to meet Prophet physically. Gently sing HU for a few minutes and then sing "Prophet" with love in your heart and he will respond. It may take time to recognize his presence, but it will come. The Light and Love that flows through him is the same that has flowed through all of God's true Prophets.

A more abundant life awaits you,

Prophet Del Hall III

HU — An Ancient Name For God

HU is an ancient name for God that can be sung quietly or aloud in prayer. HU has existed since the beginning of time in one form or another and is available to all regardless of religion. It is a pure way to express your love to God and give thanks for your blessings.

Singing HU (HUUUUUU pronounced "hue") serves as a tuning fork with Spirit that brings you into greater harmony with the Divine. We recommend singing HU a few minutes each day. This can bring love, joy, peace, and clarity, or help you rise to a higher view of a situation when upset or fearful.

Articles of Faith

Written by Prophet Del Hall III

1. There is one true God who is still living and active in our lives. He is knowable and wants a relationship with each of His children. He is the same God Jesus called FATHER and is known by many names, including Heavenly Father, and the ancient names for God, HU, and Sugmad (Pronounced SOOG-mahd). God wants a loving, trusting, personal relationship with each of us, NOT one based upon fear or guilt.

2. The Holy Spirit is God's expression in all the worlds. It is in two parts, the Light and the Sound. It is through His Holy Spirit God communicates and delivers all His gifts: peace, clarity, love, joy, healings, correction,

guidance, wisdom, comfort, truth, dreams, new revelations, and more.

3. God always has a chosen living Prophet to teach His ways, speak His Living Word, lift up Souls, and bring us closer to God. God's living Prophet is a concentrated aspect of the Holy Spirit, the Light and Sound, and is raised up and ordained by God directly. His Prophet is empowered and authorized to share God's Light and Sound and to correct misunderstandings of His ways. There are two aspects of God's Prophet, an inner spiritual and outer physical Prophet. The inner Prophet can teach us through dreams, intuition, spiritual travel, inner communication, and his presence. The outer Prophet also teaches through his discourses, written word, and his presence. There is no separation between the inner and outer Prophet. Both inner and outer aspects of Prophet are concentrated aspects of the Holy Spirit. Prophet is always with us spiritually on

the inner. Prophet points to and glorifies the Father.

4. God so loves the world and His children He has always had a long unbroken line of His chosen Prophets on Earth. They existed before Jesus and after Jesus. Jesus was God's Prophet and His actual SON. God's chosen Prophets are considered to be in the "role of God's son," though NOT literally His Son. Only Jesus was literally His Son. Prophets were sometimes called Paraclete. The Bible uses the word Comforter, but the original Greek word was Paraclete, which is more accurate. Paraclete implies an actual physical person who helps, counsels, encourages, advocates, comforts, sets free, and more.

5. Our real and eternal self is called Soul. We are Soul; we do NOT "have" a Soul. As Soul we are literally an individualized piece of God's Holy Spirit, thereby divine in nature. As an individual and uniquely experienced

Soul you have free will, intelligence, imagination, opinions, clear and continuous access to Divine guidance, and immortality. As Soul we have an innate and profound spiritual growth potential. Soul has the ability to travel the Heavens spiritually with Prophet to gain truth and wisdom and grow in love. Soul exists because God loves It.

6. We have one eternal life as Soul. However, Soul needs to incarnate many times into a physical body to learn and grow spiritually mature. Soul's long journey back home to God where It was first created encompasses many lifetimes. A loving God does not expect His children to learn His ways in a single lifetime.

7. Soul equals Soul, in that God loves all Souls equally and each Soul has the same innate qualities and potential. Soul is neither male nor female, any particular race, nationality, or age. When Soul comes into a physical body at birth, the physical body is

male or female, a certain race, a nationality, and has an age. All Souls are children of God. We do not have to earn God's Love; He loves us unconditionally.

8. Soul incarnates on Earth to grow in the ability to give and receive love and learn to live the way God wishes us to live. Because God loves us, His ways of living create abundant, happy, fulfilling lives. His beautiful ways of living are mostly HOW to live, and less on what NOT to do.

9. God is more interested in two Souls learning to love one another regardless of their sexual preference. God loves you just the way you are.

10. It is God's will that a negative power exists to help Soul grow spiritually through challenges and hardships, thereby strengthening and maturing Soul. We are never given a challenge greater than our ability to find a solution to or understand the

necessary lesson, if we use our God-given creativity, make sufficient personal effort, and ask for and accept the help available from the Divine. Soul has the ability to rise above any obstacles with God's help.

11. We study the Bible as an authentic teaching tool of God's ways, in addition to books and discourses authored by a Prophet chosen by God. We know the original biblical writings are sometimes misunderstood, for example, God loves each of us regardless of our errors and shortcomings. God's eternal abandonment or damnation is not true. He would never turn His back to us for eternity. (Isaiah 54:7-8 and 10, Lamentations 3:31-32, and Hebrews 13:5)

12. Karma is the way in which the Divine accounts for our actions, words, thoughts, and attitudes. One can create positive or negative karma. Karma is a blessing used to teach us responsibility.

13. A child is not born in sin, however, the child does have karma from former lives. Karma, God's accounting system, explains our birth circumstances better than the concept of sin.

14. A living Prophet, including Jesus, can remove karma and sin when necessary to help us get started or to grow on the path home to God. However, it is primarily our responsibility to live and grow in the ways of God, thereby not creating negative karma and sin.

15. There are four commandments of God in which we abide: First — Love God with all your heart, mind, and Soul; Second — Love your neighbor as yourself. The Third is, "Seek ye first the Kingdom of God, and His righteousness." This means that it is primarily our responsibility to draw close to God, learn His ways, and strive to live the way God would like us to live. God's Prophet is sent to show His ways. Our purpose, the Fourth

Commandment, is to become spiritually mature to be used by God to bless His children. Becoming a coworker with God through His Comforter is our primary purpose in life and the most rewarding attainment of Soul.

16. All Souls upon translation, death of the physical body, go to the higher worlds, called Heavens, planes, or mansions, regardless of their beliefs. The way they live life on Earth and the effort made to draw close to God impacts the area of Heaven they are to be sent. Those who purposely harm others (except in defense of self or others), themselves, or live against the ways of God go to unpleasant locations on the first Heaven; to a location where they can learn how to do better, as a gift of love. The first Heaven has a wide range of locations, from very very unpleasant and hellish, to wonderful and beautiful places to spend time with loved ones while learning and preparing

for future incarnations. Those who draw close to a Prophet of God, including Jesus, receive special care. We know of twelve distinct Heavens, not one. The primary Abode of the Heavenly Father is in the twelfth Heaven, known as the Ocean of Love and Mercy. We can visit God while we still live on Earth, if taken by His chosen Prophet and only as Soul, not in a physical body.

17. Prayer is sacred, personal exchange with God and is an extreme privilege. God hears every prayer from the heart whether or not we recognize a response. Singing an ancient name of God, HU, is our foundational prayer. It expresses love and gratitude to God and is unencumbered by words. Singing HU has the potential to raise us up in consciousness making us more receptive to God's Love, Light, and guiding Hand. After praying it is best to spend time listening to God. Prayer should never be rote or routine. We desire to trust God and to know His will for us, and

then freely and joyfully surrender to His will rather than our own will. God's Prophet can teach us the "Language of the Divine" which will help us understand how God communicates with us and help us recognize God's Love in our lives.

18. It is our responsibility to stay spiritually nourished. When Soul is nourished and fortified It becomes activated, and we are more receptive and have clearer communication with the Divine. When Jesus said, "Give us this day our daily bread," he meant daily spiritual nourishment, not physical bread. The Holy Spirit is nourishment for Soul. This can be received by singing HU, studying Scripture, praying, dream study, demonstrating gratitude for our blessings, being in a living Prophet's physical presence or in his inner presence, or listening to his words.

19. TRUTH has the power to improve every area of our lives, but only if understood, accepted, and integrated into our lives.

20. God and His Prophet guide us in our sleeping dreams and awake dreams as a gift of love. God's Prophet teaches how to understand both types of dreams. All areas of our lives may be blessed by the wisdom God offers each of us directly in dreams.

21. Gratitude is extremely important on the path of love. It is literally the secret of love. Developing an attitude of gratitude is necessary to becoming spiritually mature. Recognizing and being grateful for the blessings of God in our lives is vital to building a loving and trusting relationship with God and His chosen Prophet. A relationship with God's Prophet is THE KEY to everything good. This includes a more abundant life filled with the Treasures of Heaven Jesus taught about in Matthew 6.

22. We are to be good stewards of our blessings. We recognize them as gifts of love from God and make the effort to have remembrance. Remembering our blessings helps to keep our hearts open to God and builds trust in God's Love for us.

23. We give others the respect and freedom to have their own beliefs, make their own choices, and live their lives as they wish. We expect the same in return.

24. The Love and blessings of God and His Prophet are available to all who are receptive. If one desires guidance and help from Prophet, ask from the heart and sing "Prophet." He will respond. One does not need to meet Prophet physically to receive help because he is a concentrated aspect of God's Holy Spirit, and is always with us. To be taught by Prophet in the physical is a sacred blessing. Much can be gained by reading or listening to the Heavenly Father's teachings being shared by Prophet.

25. We have a responsibility to do our part and let God and His Prophet do their part. This responsibility brings freedom. Our goal is to remain spiritually nourished, live the ways of God, live in balance with a core peace, and serve God as a coworker through His Comforter. We pray to use our God-given free will in a way that our actions, thoughts, words, and attitudes testify and bear witness to the Glory and Love of God.

26. There is always more to learn and grow in God's ways and truth. One cannot remain the same spiritually. One must make the effort to move forward or risk falling backward. To grow in consciousness and love requires change. Spiritual wisdom gained during our earthly incarnations can be taken to the other worlds when we translate, and into future lifetimes, unlike our physical possessions that remain in the physical.

Contact Information

Guidance for a Better Life is a worldwide mentoring program provided by Prophet Del Hall III and his son Del Hall IV. Personal one-on-one mentoring at our retreat center is our premier offering and the most direct and effective way to grow spiritually. Spiritual tools, guided exercises, and in-depth discourses on the eternal teachings of God are provided to help one become more aware of and receptive to His Holy Spirit and the abundance that awaits. With this personally-tailored guidance one begins to more fully recognize God's Love daily in their lives, both the dramatic and the very subtle. Over time our mentoring reduces fear, worry, anxiety, lack of purpose, feelings of unworthiness, guilt, and confusion; replacing those negative aspects of life with an abundance of peace, clarity, joy, wisdom, love, and self-respect leading to a more personal relationship with God, more than most know is possible. We also offer our videos, and more than twenty inspirational and educational books.

Guidance for a Better Life
P.O. Box 219
Lyndhurst, Virginia 22952
(540) 377-6068
contact@guidanceforabetterlife.com
www.guidanceforabetterlife.com

"A Growing Testament to the Power of God's Love One Profound Book at a Time."

If you could only read one of Prophet Del Hall's books this is the one. It is full of Keys to unlock the treasures of Heaven and bring more of God's Love into your life.

Wayshowers are God's special emissaries to Earth. Our Heavenly Father loves us so much He has never left us alone without a Wayshower to teach us His true ways. This book explores the amazing history of God's chosen and ordained Wayshowers from thirty-five thousand years ago to today through specific examples of both well-known and little-known Wayshowers.

GOD IS IN THE GARDEN PARABLES

Regardless of what your venture is in life you can benefit from this unassuming book. It may appear small, but the parables contained within have the power to affect your life in extraordinary ways.

ZOOM WITH PROPHET

Guidance for a Better Life retreat center has been hosting in-person mountaintop retreats at our beautiful location in the Blue Ridge Mountains of Virginia since 1990. When the pandemic began in 2020, it inspired us to get creative with how to connect with our students and new seekers. It was then our *Zoom With Prophet* meeting series was born. Some of these Zoom meetings are now being put into book form for those who could not attend.

SPECIALIZED TOPICS

Whether you wish to reconnect with a loved one who has passed, understand how you too can experience God's Light, improve your marriage, or learn how to understand your dreams, these incredible books have you covered.

TESTIMONIES OF GOD'S LOVE SERIES

God expresses His Love every day in many different and sometimes subtle ways. Often this love goes unrecognized because the ways in which God communicates are not well known. Each of the books in this series contains fifty true stories that will help you learn to better recognize the Love of God in your life.

JOURNEY TO A TRUE SELF-IMAGE SERIES

This series includes intimate and unique stories that many readers will be able to personally identify with, enjoy, and learn from. They will help the reader transcend the false images people often carry about themselves — first and foremost that they are only their physical mind and body. The authors share their journeys of recognizing and coming to more fully accept their true self-image, that of Soul — an eternal child of God.

www.ingramcontent.com/pod-product-compliance
Lightning Source LLC
Chambersburg PA
CBHW071509040426
42444CB00008B/1564